What the Doctor Orders

To contact Howard Manns, Author and Speaker,
for training, conferences or speaking engagements
email: Howard@howardmanns.com

Howard J. Manns
1076 High Meadows Drive
Gibsonia, PA 15044
724-816-7801
howard@howardmanns.com

www.phdmkt.com
www.howardmanns.com

Patient Name:_____

Address:_____Date:_____

R_X

WHAT THE
DOCTOR
ORDERS

What Every Health Care
Professional NEEDS to Know
about Marketing to Physicians

MD:_____

Signature:_____

by

Howard Manns

Copyright © 2014 Lynward Publishing
ISBN: 978-0-9906201-0-5

Professional Healthcare Development
1076 High Meadows Drive
Gibsonia, Pennsylvania 15044
Office: 724-816-7801
Cell: 412-855-0619
Fax: 1-866-881-2883

Website: www.phdmkt.com
Email: howard@phdmkt.com

Editor: Kathleen Dixon Donnelly
kaydee@gypsyteacher.com

Book cover design: Joseph Cancilla

Book interior design: Jean Boles
http://jeanboles.elance.com

Acknowledgements

Special thanks to the physicians, administrators and discharge planners who participated in providing the information necessary to create this publication.

A special thank you to Pam Brossman, ten times #1 best- selling author, and CEO of PamBrossman.com for her optimism, guidance, and inspiration that encouraged me to become a published author.

CONTENTS

INTRODUCTION

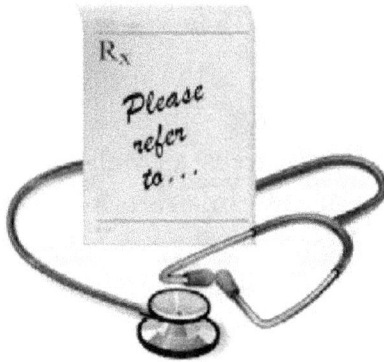

The world of healthcare marketing has become increasingly more difficult, more crowded, more challenging and more of all the other elements that once made this an exciting career. While it's still exciting for the ambitious-at-heart marketer, a more strategic approach is needed to be successful.

The increasingly competitive landscape of the industry is driving the need to re-evaluate how a company delivers their message to the referral source with any hope of getting a return on the investment. Building relationships is still the number one tactic to creating a successful referral network, but due to the state of technology and the healthcare industry's ever-changing platforms, it's important to know how to make the most of every minute of an interaction with a referral source. Technology will never replace the face-to-face meeting and handshake of a personal relationship. Technology is a tool, and not an option when building relationships. This is especially important when marketing to physicians. Whether general practitioners or specialists, their time is limited and your time to make an impact is more limited as a result.

What the Doctor Orders is the result of a six-month study conducted in mid-2013. Interviews were held with physician referral resources as well as nursing home and personal care home administrators to find out what they would like to tell marketers such as yourself who call on them for business. While the list of questions for each interview was lengthy, the replies were summed up in the following question:

"If you could say something to healthcare marketers regarding their relationship with you, what would it be?"

While many of the answers should come as no surprise to seasoned marketers, it was interesting to hear a few twists in the way marketers are perceived and, more importantly, how easy it can be to improve the process. A list of all the interview questions appears in Appendix A for your reference. The book is laid out in a way that summarizes the overall results of the interviews, and each of the eight sections includes some great ideas on how you can meet their expectations while delivering your message.

CHAPTER ONE:

On Research and Background

QUESTION: *How important is it for your marketer to REALLY know your business before they meet with you? Can you tell if they're green?*

The implication here is that physicians aren't interested in hearing what you have to say if they have to educate you about their business. If you don't know anything about the person you're meeting, there's not much room to discuss anything relevant. Who does this physician primarily service? Who do they currently refer to on a regular basis and why? A physician's clientele may be from a lower income area or a higher income area–each target has different needs. And what about the insurance? What can they take? What is their affiliation?

If you don't know anything about the person you're meeting, there's not much room to discuss anything relevant.

RESPONSE #1:

"Yes, they really need to know my business. I can tell if they're green about their own business as well. Please know what you're talking about."

As one physician put it, if the marketer doesn't know much about their own business, how can they explain it to someone else? It's easy to identify someone who is nervous and unclear about insurance, qualifications, admission policies, etc., by the way they present themselves.

RESPONSE #2:

"A marketer should know the type of clientele that I service."

The best marketers have a superior knowledge of their customers.

How can you do research about the physician? In today's social media world it's easier than ever before. The first step would be to simply "Google" their name and see what you get. Usually you'll find their or their practice's website. Never stop at the first page of results—continue your search for at least five pages. Sometimes you'll find awards and recognitions from years past. You can also find out if they have any affiliations with other organizations.

Your next search should include LinkedIn—a great business site for professionals. If they have put up a profile, you can read their biography and background, giving you an immense amount of research and discussion material. LinkedIn also includes different group memberships and other links that may provide you with additional insight. And don't forget to search other members of the physician group such as nurses, administrative assistants, clinical staff and so on. I once researched a physician and found out that he was a musician. Because I have a strong background as a musician/songwriter, the relationship was an easy one to develop.

The key is to go into the meeting armed with information to carry on an intelligent conversation. Remember, your goal is to build a relationship.

RESPONSE #3:
"Do your research! Know the hierarchy of my office."

More than one interviewee pointed out that a marketer should know the hierarchy of the office: Who makes the referrals? Who is the administrative assistant? Are there several nurses? Who is the office manager? These are key people if you plan on getting an appointment with the physician.

RESPONSE #4:
"They should know and understand my regulations."
—Nursing Home Administrators/Personal Care Home Administrators ((NHA/PCHA).

Interviews with long-term care administrators often yielded the same answers, with some variations. One of these was the comment that the marketer should have a basic understanding of the regulations governing an assisted living facility. As an administrator myself I can tell you that I am always impressed with someone who understands my challenges when it comes to admissions. One example is hospice marketing. The regulations state that the facility must have a hospice license on file if that hospice is servicing the facility. A new certificate is needed each year. One hospice company I worked with used the opportunity to hand-deliver that license each year and provided me with information about key changes to help me understand their process better. Who do you think I referred to on a regular basis?

Research is a critical strategy and the tactics are numerous. It's important that you really know your business and that of your referral source if you want to be an exceptional marketer who appears as a breath of fresh air to any referral group.

The Prescription:

Patient Name:
Address: Date:

R_X

SCRIPT ONE:
Understand the
physician's
clientele

MD:
Signature:

Are they rich or poor? What is their ethnicity and culture? What is the use cycle of your service? Demographic research can be free and available from census sites with the help of a friendly librarian.

Understand that you are meeting with a well-educated and clinically experienced individual. Don't waste time telling them what they already know.

Patient Name:_____
Address:_____ Date:_____

R℞

SCRIPT TWO: Know the hierarchy of the referral practice

MD:_____
Signature:_____

Find out who actually does the referral. Get a connection with the receptionist or administrative assistant in the office. This person usually knows everybody's business.

Patient Name:_____
Address:_____ Date:_____

R
X

**SCRIPT THREE:
Have a basic
understanding of
their regulations**

MD:_____
Signature:_____

This gives you the edge and shows your interest in their business. Read the violation report of assisted living/nursing homes; this is always available, as it is required to be accessible to the public. This will give you some topics to discuss and an opportunity to offer your services such as training, etc.

CHAPTER TWO:

On Relationships and Becoming a Resource

QUESTION: *How important is your relationship with a marketer?*

Your first impression on them is lasting and sets up the possibility for future meetings. And you never get a second chance to make a first impression.

Healthcare marketing is all about the relationship—it's that simple. People like to work with people they like. Communication and building rapport is key. In his book, *Everyone Communicates, Few Connect*, leadership author

John Maxwell asks the question, "Are you communicating or are you connecting?" All of the respondents to our interviews made it clear that having a relationship with the marketer is important.

RESPONSE #1:
 "It's important that I know where AND who I am sending my patient to. I have to have a bond at some level."

The last section stressed the importance of researching your referral sources to the point of stalking. Let's talk about using that information to build the all-important relationship–the lifeblood of all referral programs.

All referral sources have one need in common–the need for trust. Trust is the cornerstone in patient-centered care for referrals. The physicians were all in agreement on this. They insisted on knowing where and to whom they were sending their patients. "The only way that can happen is by having some sort of bond," stated one PCP.

RESPONSE #2:
"I don't care how much they know, I need to know how much they care. There has to be a connection for that to happen."

How can you start a relationship with someone you don't know? Find common terrain. There's no better way than to find something in common with someone—something as simple as graduating from the same college, sharing a musical or literary interest, or having children playing the same sport. In addition to internet research and social networking groups such as LinkedIn, what about primary research opportunities?

Let me explain with a personal example.
Several years ago I was a marketing director for a Continuing Care Retirement Community (CCRC). The local hospital was one of the main referral resources for our community but, due to a challenging past history and a difficult director in charge of all discharges [We'll call him Albert for the purpose of this story.], it didn't seem that they knew we existed. As the new marketing director (there had been at least three before me over the past year), I had my work cut out for me. I had to begin with the hospital if I was going to get any impressive results.

I thought a direct approach would work so decided to stop by to introduce myself. But I was in for my first disappointment. As I walked down the hall in the hospital I saw Albert, who very quickly ducked into his office and closed the door as soon as he realized who I was. It was obvious that no one got to see the great Oz. Being the optimist, I attempted several times over the next week to get into see him but my visits were met with a similar scenario each time—closed door, no appointments available. I decided on a more strategic approach of mapping out his habits and building relationships with some of the staff to find out everything I could about his likes, dislikes and daily routine.

On one of my visits, I caught a quick glimpse of Albert's office and noticed the key to my common thread with him— a Beatle poster. A devout Beatle fanatic myself, I formulated a plan. Finally able to catch Albert one morning,

I said, "Hi, I see you're a Beatle fan. Can you answer a riddle?" I asked him the question and, he answered quickly with pride. He returned a question to me to check how astute I was with Beatle trivia. My response was, "Wow, can I get back to you on that one? That could be a trick question!" He smiled as if he'd won a grand prize and agreed to give me a chance to research the answer and get back to him.

I had just earned myself a trip back to the hospital to meet my new best friend and prove my Beatle-worthiness. A strategy had begun. It wasn't long before Albert and I formed a bond based on the Fab Four. He even called me one morning around six o'clock to stop over and have coffee with him.

Through a connection to a topic totally unrelated to healthcare I was able to build an all-important relationship. The result? The hospital became one of our best referral sources to build our census. The power of a relationship can't be topped.

You may find that stalking, mapping out habits, and following someone's daily routine might be right out of an episode of CSI. But this is a strategy and a process. It's not a haphazard, hit or miss program.

RESPONSE #3:
"Yes, a relationship is important, but don't try to rush this process."

Another point that came across loud and clear among all the respondents (physicians, discharge planners, and facility administrators alike) was the pace of relationship building. It's impossible to build a relationship in one or two visits. They considered acting as though you are "old friends" from the start feels fake and pompous, completely breaking the first rule of gaining trust. Take your time and find some connection. You'll know when the time is right by the tone of the discussions you are having.

The best way to strategically plan is to ask yourself questions regarding your meeting with the referral source: Is your communication personal? Do you ask specific questions about matters of interest to the source? Is your focus on their needs or yours? If you are seeking information, are you explaining why you need it? What is your value to this person?

RESPONSE #4:
"I look for a resource—someone who I can trust to provide me with great service as well as information."

While providing the best service is always a retention factor in keeping the business, physicians are more likely to deal with those who can demonstrate how their service can complement (and benefit) the physician's practice.

Another way to build a relationship with referral sources is to become an invaluable information resource for them. All of the participants in this survey are busy professionals who don't have a lot of time to keep up with industry trends. Although the internet has made research easier, there's too much information to sort through to even get topline details. Go ahead—type in "Healthcare Marketing" to Google and you get 2.7 million hits. This presents a huge opportunity for you to provide your referral with well-organized, bullet-pointed information.

RESPONSE #5:
"We are very time-challenged and it's getting worse with the aging population. I would welcome any published data. Just refer me to the resource."

Several of the physicians I spoke with mentioned that they would appreciate a top-line summary of information that is interesting to them. Providing an industry White Paper could be the key that sets you apart.

A White Paper is an in-depth report on a topic or series of topics. You could also write your own on a relevant topic that you have researched or are already expert in. You can learn more about White Papers by going to

http://coe.winthrop.edu/educ651/readings/HowTo_White Paper.pdf.

Because a White Paper could be anywhere from two to 15 pages, or even more, it is best to provide a cover page with three to four bullet points outlining the key facts and clear subheads throughout. Busy people appreciate a large quantity of helpful information, as long as it is well organized and well presented. Include a reference to the online resources you used in case they want to learn more, but be sure to include your own contact details as well.

You might want to attach to the cover a thank you letter following your visit. Below is a sample follow-up cover sheet.

Dear Dr. Smith,

Thank you for taking time out of your day to meet with me last week. I appreciate your confidence in me and your trust in my office by referring Gertrude Fagan. We look forward to providing her the same level of care she is used to from your office.

As a follow up to our conversation about recent break-throughs in the healthcare system, I've attached some articles I found. A quick topline of the information is as follows:

✓ New Insights into Dementia

A medical research team may have found a major pathway leading to brain cell death in mice, and used an oral compound to block it. The treatment stopped the disease in its tracks,

✓ Parkinson's & Alzheimer's: Green Tea May Hold Answers

Medical researchers are seeing a much brighter future for victims of Parkinson's, Alzheimer's and other neuro-degenerative diseases.

✓ Sleep Research

We spend a third of our lives sleeping. But for a large percentage of the adult population, sleep disturbances are common. New breakthrough studies may have the answer.

Again, thank you for your time and referral. If I can be of any assistance to you or your staff, please contact me at 000-000-0000 or call the number on the attached card.

Sincerely,

Mary J. Marketer
Clinical Liaison
XYZ Company

The Prescription

Patient Name:_____
Address:_____ Date:_____

R_X

SCRIPT ONE:
Find common
terrain (music,
sports, book, etc.)

MD:_____
Signature:_____

The best relationships start by finding something in common with the person you're meeting with. Talk to their administrative assistant and staff members, and look on social media sites such as LinkedIn or Google. Connecting can be even more important than communicating.

Patient Name:_____
Address:_____ Date:_____

R℞

SCRIPT TWO:
Become a
resource

MD:_____
Signature:_____

Once you find common terrain, provide information that would interest your referral source. This could include White Papers, periodicals, information about advances in healthcare, hard-to-find data, or a "Top 10 List of Fun Facts" about a topic they are interested in.

Patient Name:_____
Address:_____ Date:_____

R℞

SCRIPT THREE:
Planning and
strategies takes
time

MD:_____
Signature:_____

Relationships are built after three to four encounters on average. Don't rush the process! When you meet someone for the first time, listening and focus should be your primary goal. My best meetings have always been the ones that I don't talk much or try to "make the sale."

CHAPTER THREE:

On Timing and First Impressions

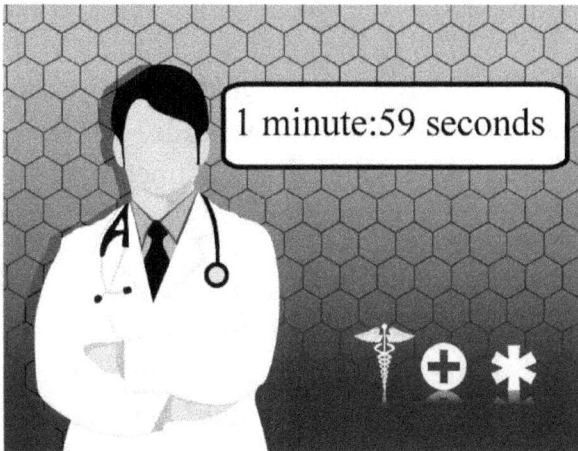

QUESTION: *When you meet with a marketer, how much time do you typically allow?*

In almost all of the interviews, the time constraints of the physicians and administrators were brought up whether I asked about them or not. This is one reason why your first impression on them is lasting and can set up the possibility for future meetings. And you never get a second chance to make a first impression.

RESPONSE #1:

"We have approximately seven to ten minutes per patient, so it's unrealistic for me to give a marketer more than five minutes. It's important that the marketer has a plan. I can tell in two minutes if I'm willing to give five minutes."

You are trying to build a relationship, not sell a service. It all comes down to providing value to your referral source. Research is the key. You are not the only marketer who will be visiting them this week. It's important that you stand out.

Do you know about the four-second rule? When you first meet someone, they make a judgment about you within the first four seconds. But here's what is really scary: For the remaining time after the four seconds—which could be up to five or 10 minutes—the person is unconsciously trying to justify what they felt about you in that first four seconds. Prepare well for that first impression!

You've seen commercials for new movies, often called trailers. These are seldom longer than 90 seconds to two minutes and are designed to catch your attention and get you to want to see the movie. The same goes for your first impression with a physician or referral source.

Like the movie trailer, your goal is to make them want to spend more time with you in the future, through a second appointment which will start to build a relationship.

RESPONSE #2:

"If they've taken the time to schedule a meeting with me ahead of time, I typically keep it to ten minutes. But if it's pre-packaged, it's less."

What does "pre-packaged" mean? One physician told me that a marketer came in, sat down, opened up their own brochure and began reading it. You would never do that. But obviously somebody did. Pre-packaged is just another way of describing a canned speech, so prepared that it doesn't seem sincere. It sounds as though you're reading a script that could have been written to be delivered to anyone, not the very important person you are talking to.

Your 30-second elevator pitch, as it is sometimes called, needs to be enticing, inviting, and interesting. What I've learned from these interviews is that most of us don't spend enough time preparing for the meetings. Even if you are a natural at being personable, you still need to practice.

The 30-second elevator speech is more like a movie trailer--a short clip that makes the viewer want to go to the movie and see it. In your case, you have to provide quick snippets in your introduction speech that will make the physician (or referral source) want to hear more. Adding items such as 24-hour access to you, the marketer may be the edge you need since returning calls and answering on the first few rings have become a lost art.

RESPONSE #3:
"Even with a pre-scheduled meeting, there has to be value if you want me to spend any more than five minutes. I have far too many corporate commitments." - (NHA/PCHA)

This response came from some of the administrators I spoke with. Understanding your referral source's daily commit-ments and constraints will demonstrate to them that you understand their business.

For example, unless a meeting is pre-scheduled, you should never attempt a first meeting on a Monday or a Friday. Mondays are usually full of reports, weekend recaps, and other issues; Fridays are wrap-up before heading for home.

The Prescription

Patient Name:_____
Address:_____ Date:_____

R_x

**SCRIPT ONE:
Review your
elevator pitch
and make sure
it has impact**

MD:_____
Signature:_____

Remember the four-second rule. Are you interesting enough for a second appointment? Be prepared to demonstrate that time spent with you has value. You have two minutes to perform. Practice! Practice! Practice!

Patient Name:_____
Address:_____ Date:_____

R_x

**SCRIPT TWO:
Develop a
profile on each
referral source**

MD:_____
Signature:_____

Relationships take time. Track each visit and form a strategy for the next. It's impossible to remember every detail about someone, especially when you've got a large clientele. What are their likes? Dislikes? What are your common bonds? (See Appendix B for a sample Profile Sheet.)

Patient Name:_____
Address:_____ Date:_____

R͓x

SCRIPT THREE:
Use Mondays and
Fridays to plan or
recap your week

MD:_____
Signature:_____

On these days don't visit busy referral sources unless you have pre-scheduled appointments. Your goal is to become a resource, not a nuisance. Timing is everything.

BONUS SECTION:

Getting Past the Gatekeeper

One of the most common occurrences in your life as a healthcare marketer—and also your worst nightmare— is getting past the gatekeeper. Whether at a physician's office, a nursing home, or the hospital administrative department, this doesn't have to be difficult. Like every other strategy in marketing, first you need a plan to get to the decision-maker.

The following is a short list of six strategies I've collected while conducting these interviews:

Tool up

"We have approximately seven to ten minutes per patient, so it's unrealistic for me to give more than five minutes to a salesman. It's important that the marketer has a plan. I can tell in two minutes if I'm willing to give five minutes."

When visiting an office in person, it's important to understand your own strengths and use all the tools in your arsenal. If you're tall, use it to your benefit. If you have an executive look, your appearance will work in your favor as well. If people see you as important, they will treat you that way. You will always dress professionally, of course, but also use a relaxed and calm voice. Speak slowly and articulately. Don't divulge any more information than necessary. Remember that the gatekeeper is not the decision-maker in most cases. Your "packaging" is important and the first opening seconds of your conversation with the gatekeeper may make all the difference.

Get the name of the decision-maker from the gatekeeper.

"Treat my staff (administrative assistant, receptionist) with respect or you'll never get in the door again. They are the ones you'll be working with more often."

The biggest mistake is not asking for the right person. Do your research, including searching Google, talking to other

WHAT THE DOCTOR ORDERS

marketers who have already gotten past the gatekeeper, or, as a last resort, simply asking the gatekeeper. Remember that the receptionist, administrative assistant, etc., sees an average of six to 10 marketers per day. Gatekeepers can be a wealth of knowledge but they get to practice their approach with intruders every day. Ask simple, open questions to build up a picture of both the gatekeeper and the decision-maker. They are not the enemy and in many cases are well-respected by the decision-maker.

The gatekeeper is seldom the decision-maker

Gatekeepers have many strengths, but they do not hold decision-making powers. Don't try to pitch your product or service to them; it will waste your time. More importantly, it will waste their time, which is very irritating to busy people who will look for any opportunity to tell you that they cannot help you. While it's important to build a relationship with the gatekeeper, it is hard to do if you act as though you are desperate.

Slow down

We live in a fast-paced society. As marketers, our quest to "make the numbers" can force us to rush through every process. If you are stressed, tense, in a hurry, or even just nervous, you will transfer those feelings in voice tone and body language onto the gatekeeper. All of this will have an impact on their perception of you and your service. Take a few deep breaths, smile, and confidently greet your gatekeeper with calm, positive energy.

Ditch the script

> *"Too much talk and not enough listening. Canned speeches. If they would only let me talk while they listen, instead of preparing a response while I'm speaking."*

Unless you were recently nominated for an Oscar and are considered a really good actor, don't use a prepared script on gatekeepers. They've heard it all before. Instead, spend some time on an individual plan for each facility or service. This includes finding out all you can about their gatekeepers. Anticipate their responses to your inquiry and plan your responses to any key objections. Remember that your first goal is to build a relationship with the person who will get you in to see the decision-maker.

Don't avoid or evade the gatekeeper

Don't try to sneak past these important people. You'll get cut off at the ankles and ruin your chances of building a relationship with that person. The moment you learn the gatekeeper's name, write it down and start addressing him or her personally. You should be using their name at least two times during each conversation. You need to engage gatekeepers without getting too personal or appear to be prying. While it's unlikely that you'll become best friends (although I've seen this happen), building a strong rapport with these all-important individuals will make them want to help you.

Some gatekeepers are difficult to crack. They are simply doing their job of blocking unwanted visits and interruptions from external forces interfering with their boss' daily routine.

If you do come across a gatekeeper who just doesn't seem possible to get past, as a last resort consider calling during off hours such as early mornings, lunch times, or after-hours.

> *"Follow-up is one of the most important parts of this process, especially with my office and support staff. Also, be honest if something goes wrong. Things happen."*

Throughout this book, I've consistently talked about follow-up. This is just as important with gatekeepers. Assistants and receptionists usually don't get a lot of recognition. Send a simple thank you note, or a small token of appreciation, like a cup with calming tea, etc. You'll win them over the next time you stop by.

CHAPTER FOUR:

On Presentation and Communication

> *The art of listening is a two-part skill.*
> *A) Listening to what they are saying, and*
> *B) Making the person feel that you are listening!*

QUESTION: *What is the one thing that makes you decide to not meet a second time with a marketer?*

The answer to this question was unanimous across the board. The focus was consistently on communication skills, including body language, tone of voice, and general attitude of the marketer to everyone in the office.

RESPONSE #1:
"Too much talk and not enough listening. Canned speeches. If they would only let me talk while they listen, instead of preparing a response while I'm speaking."

When listeners listen, talkers will talk. In the book *Managing Expectations: Working with People Who Want More, Better, Faster, Sooner, Now!* Naomi Karten identifies an additional trait: The skill of *showing* people that you are listening. Have you ever had a conversation with someone who is typing on their computer while they are "listening" to you? Did you think they were really listening? You may think that you can listen while doing something else, but their perception will be that you are much more interested in what you are doing than what they are saying.

Learn to listen – opportunity sometimes knocks very softly.

If you're not listening you won't pick up clues on how you can deliver value to this referral source. If this isn't easy for you, practice asking questions which will force you to listen for the answer. Clarity is king! If a referred patient/resident is scheduled to use your services or go to your facility, never assume the time and date. Get the details! Or ask the physician for a contact person who can provide you with the details. In the course of developing a relationship, listening demonstrates interest and is one of the best ways to build trust and rapport. If you provide ancillary services—transportation, family consultations, etc.—by listening you can pick up on additional services that the referral may need but is not aware that you supply.

A Word about Expectations

Managing expectations is one of the secrets to marketing success. The better you know your referral source, the better you'll be in tune with what they expect.

To be a great people-person marketer, you need to first understand expectations and then manage them on a regular basis. Why? Because as people change so do their expectations. This book was developed to help healthcare marketers like you with the general expectations of common referral sources. It's a personal process and everyone is unique.

Sometimes your referral source's expectations of you seem unreasonable. In their eyes, your expectations of them may be equally unreasonable. Failure to manage this aspect of the relationship may cause serious problems.

Expectations are influenced by a wide array of factors. This includes your referral's belief system, past experience with you or your competition, false assumptions, management styles, and modes of operation. To be successful in today's minute-by-minute information transfer, you need to do your homework and research.

RESPONSE #2:
"Be authentic. Sell me on the relationship, not the product or service. Sometimes we just want to complain—listen!"

Nobody wants to be sold, but everyone wants to be helped. –John Maxwell

The most common symptom of poor listening is concentrating on composing a response to their question or comment instead of truly listening to what they are telling you. One key sign that you have a good relationship developing is when your meeting becomes more conversational and less formally business-oriented. This should be your goal. Some of the best communicators in history were known to say very few words.

While listening is the most important message here, you still need to be able to respond intelligently. If you're good with instant responses, that's not a problem. If not, spend some time anticipating questions you may be asked and make notes of your answers in advance. The more appointments you have, the easier it will be to develop a fairly accurate list. Have another member of your team come up with some potential questions, and critique the answers you prepare.

RESPONSE #3:
"Treat my staff (administrative assistants, receptionists, etc.) with respect or you'll never get in the door again. They are the ones you'll be working with more often."

I can't stress enough the importance of marketing to the entire practice. The staff provides the service in most cases, and they are gatekeepers for their supervisors. The physician or administrator makes the decisions, but is strongly influenced by the people he or she works with every day.

You can't build a relationship with everybody in the room if you don't care about anybody in the room. – John Maxwell

If the staff doesn't want to work with you, it will be obvious and your tenure will be short-lived. People like to work with people they like. And good leaders want to keep their staff happy.

Let me explain with a personal example.

Years ago, as an administrator at a personal care home, I was in the process of hiring a new director of nursing. One of the interviews was with an individual who I thought would fit well with my team. I was ready to make the offer later that day. However, I found out that, while this applicant was waiting to meet with me, she was abrasive to my administrative assistant. Despite the fact that her knowledge, clinical expertise, and salary expectations were all what we were looking for, I bypassed this individual due to her treatment of my staff.

Marketing to the whole practice can also present an opportunity for you to become another resource for the practice—perhaps as a staff trainer?

The Prescription

Patient Name:_____
Address:_____Date:_____

R~X~

SCRIPT ONE: Practice your presentation

MD:_____
Signature:_____

You won't get a second chance to make a first impression that demonstrates your knowledge and is worth listening to. Practicing should include checking your body language. Present in front of a mirror and in front of someone from your team. Do you look convincing? Ask for an honest critique. Emotions come out in the face and they are difficult to hide.

People may hear your words, but they feel your attitude. – John Maxwell

Patient Name:_____
Address:_____Date:_____

R~X~

SCRIPT TWO: Build relationships with everyone in the practice

MD:_____
Signature:_____

Pay special attention to the gatekeepers. They hold the keys. Marketing is customer service—everyone is involved.

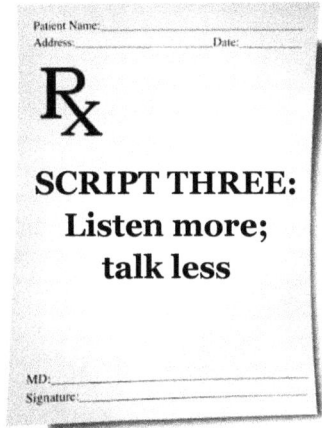

Patient Name:_____
Address:_____Date:_____

R℞x

SCRIPT THREE:
Listen more;
talk less

MD:_____
Signature:_____

Listening is a skill. Equally important is making people *feel* that you are listening. Everything you do communicates. Be conscious of your appearance, body language, tone of voice, etc.

CHAPTER FIVE:

On Lunch & Learns and Other Educational Opportunities

QUESTION: *"How do you feel about initial Lunch & Learn sessions at your office?"*

We've all done Lunch & Learn sessions at hospitals, physician offices, and other sites with referral sources. But sometimes we spend more time deciding what food and drink to bring and which eating utensils to use than we do on planning the actual presentation. Some of the responses from physicians show that we are falling short when it comes to the overall objective of a presentation—which is what a Lunch & Learn session is supposed to be.

RESPONSE #1:
"Believe it or not, staff development is an area that is a struggle for my practice. If you can provide in-service training, I'll be more than happy to meet with you on referrals. It's called a relationship."

Without fail, each interviewee expressed their need for staff education. Time is short in the daily operation of the physician's practice. But that doesn't mean that the need for staff education doesn't still exist.

The staff training you offer has to be interesting if you want to get in the door. The following is a list of key topics for any establishment that deals with the public. Your own research will tell you which would apply to the office you are hoping to work with:

- Handling Difficult Behaviors
- Understanding Patient Expectations
- Office Communication Tools
- Working with Families
- Customer Service and Body Language

Your topics should have substance and be interesting to your audience. Customer service, for example, is a strong category. A session on customer service and body language could be promoted as "Making a Great First Impression with your Patients." The staff will be interested and the physician will appreciate the information.

RESPONSE #2:
"If you are presenting about your business, make it about your services, not your company. My staff and my team may need to know more about homecare, hospice, or rehabilitation. Be informative."

A good marketer represents his or her company. A great marketer represents and is knowledgeable about the service they provide. Remember that your brochure is simply back up to everything you talk about during your presentation.

You should discuss breakthroughs in your industry such as new techniques in hospice care or advances in technology regarding rehabilitation services. If you are using PowerPoint or a small computer as part of your presentation, play a 30- or 60-second commercial or video about your company prior to getting into your presentation. This along with your business card and brochure leave-behind should be enough to promote your company and brand. The rest of the content should be about the service you provide.

RESPONSE #3:
"I would suggest that you really take time to evaluate what you want to get out of a Lunch & Learn. Be different. We have lunch provided on a consistent basis from one vendor or another. If you ask who brought lunch, my staff rarely remembers the company and will usually respond 'Pizza Hut.'"

A Lunch & Learn is a networking event where you are the host and the speaker. As with any such event your goal is to build relationships. And because this may be your first exposure to the referral source, it's important to be memorable.

Food will seldom make you memorable unless it's a signature item or dessert made by your facility's chef. Do you remember what you had for lunch yesterday? I didn't think so. One of the best ways to be memorable is to have a topic that is out of the ordinary but relevant to the industry. Being a personality who they will remember and enjoy will get you repeat visits and referrals. The following is a short list of topics that are not only interesting, but enticing to healthcare professionals.

"Meditation and Pain/Stress Control"
Stress. We all have it. Talking about meditation and alternate means of relieving stress would be of interest to any physician and their staff. You could include, for example, aromatherapy. If you're not an expert, bring one with you. You will be remembered.

"Healthy Foods: The 'Dirty Dozen'"
With all the focus on eating healthier these days, the "Dirty Dozen" is a list of foods known to be high in pesticides. You can easily find this information online and even bring samples of healthy foods or the "dirty dozen."

"Why Laughter Is Medicine"
Are you known for your sense of humor? If so, use it to your advantage. Not only will you provide great information on the benefits of humor, you'll also leave them laughing and improve their afternoon. Memorable? I think so.

"Simple Supplements and Benefits" or "Migraines and Magnesium"

The abundance of information out there regarding supplementation shows that there is a great deal of interest in this area. Books and websites can provide you with a list of the top five or 10 supplements. Do your research and share the information. Did you know that magnesium deficiency is a cause of migraines? I just gave you your first tip!

Additional Topic Ideas:

✓ Understanding Patient Expectations

✓ Office Communication Tools

✓ Working with Families

✓ The New LTC Resident

✓ Uncovering Hidden Skills

✓ Handling Difficult Behaviors

✓ Handling Marketers

✓ First (and Lasting) Impressions

✓ Customer Service and Physiology

✓ Office Impressions (Physician's Achilles Heel)

✓ Simple Supplements and Benefits

Using the tips from Chapter Four, make your presentation dynamic, interesting and memorable. The programs listed in this section are available for purchase in 30-minute, 60-minute and 120-minute formats including PowerPoint slides and scripting for presentation by special order.

Email Professional Healthcare Development at **seminars@phdmkt.com for details.**

The Prescription

Patient Name:_____
Address:_____Date:_____

R
X

**SCRIPT ONE:
Title your Lunch
& Learn like a
Hollywood
movie**

MD:_____
Signature:_____

Think of a Lunch & Learn the same way you think of an advertising campaign. It's more than just food. It's an event!

Patient Name:_____
Address:_____Date:_____

R
X

**SCRIPT TWO:
Consider
training the
office staff**

MD:_____
Signature:_____

It's an unmet need for the physician. The staff has to eat, don't they? This is an easy way for you to schedule your Lunch & Learn and meet with the physician by providing value.

Patient Name:_____
Address:_____ Date:_____

Rx

SCRIPT THREE:
Think
outrageous to be
memorable

MD:_____
Signature:_____

Unless you want to be thought of as "The Pizza Hut Guy" or just a quick meal, make your presentation one that they will never forget.

SPECIAL TOPIC:

A Word about Promotional Products

Those colorful coffee mugs with your logo glowing on the side—ice scrapers, calendars, magnetic sports schedules. Do they really accomplish anything for you towards building a relationship? Many hospitals and facilities even ban staff from accepting of such gifts, so be careful. Be sure that they are relevant to your audience.

Many of the physicians I met with told me that their cupboards are full of promotional coffee mugs. They said that they can always use pens and pads, but these would have no bearing on the relationship they build with the marketer.

My advice? Be memorable. Clip boards, stress balls, shopping bags with logos, and other usable items can be effective. Know your audience first. If you're going to bring a mug, make sure you include herbal teas or exotic coffees.

BONUS SECTION:

How to Conduct a Successful Lunch & Learn Presentation

"I would suggest that you really take time to evaluate what you want to get out of a Lunch & Learn. Be different. We have lunch provided on a consistent basis from one vendor or another. If you ask who brought lunch, my staff rarely remembers the company and will usually respond 'Pizza Hut.'" – Physician response to question about Lunch & Learns

Section Contents

Introduction

As healthcare marketers, our goal is to build a referral network among healthcare professionals to keep a steady stream of activity with census, patient or client growth. If you've been in the business long enough, you understand that this comes down to one major fact—relationship marketing.

By this point in the book, you are probably tired of reading, "People like to work with people they like." But your everyday family and friend relationships are proof of this. Who do you prefer to spend time with?

The goal is to get people to understand your business and services and, most importantly, how you can make their jobs easier. You can advertise, hold events, e-mail information to your prospects and even speak to different organizations. But the strongest marketing tactic is one-on-one relationship presentations.

The Lunch & Learn is a great relationship builder—if you handle it correctly.

The following pages will give you insight into this technique by providing ideas, checklists and presentation structures to get the most impact when you present to referral sources to help you grow your business and capitalize on relationship-based marketing.

The Power of "Why?"

Why? you may be asking. Because this is the most common reason advertising and marketing programs fail. Your customers are asking:

"Why should I choose you?"

"Why should I make this decision?"

"Why should I spend this money?"

"Why should I spend time reading your brochure?"

"Why should I listen to you at all?"

You need to ask the same question of your marketing efforts. Why are you sending out direct mail? Why are you visiting the hospitals? Why are you holding this Lunch & Learn?

In this section, we'll discuss the reasons why conducting a Lunch & Learn is just plain good business. This will help you focus when preparing your materials and presentation.

Three Answers to the Question, "Why am I conducting a Lunch & Learn?"

1. It's a relationship marketing opportunity.

A Lunch & Learn provides you with a great opportunity to meet quite a few referral sources at one time, in one room and, when it's a small group, in an intimate setting. If you are conducting a session with a physician group you can be specific about how your services benefit that group. The reason is to give everyone an introduction to *you*. If it is a multi-faceted group representing a variety of companies and professions, a series of one-on-one meetings should follow in the weeks immediately after the presentation with the key individuals you've identified as contacts.

2. You can present yourself as a resource.

One important factor is on the day of the presentation. You need to "walk in smart," which is another way of saying that you must present yourself as an important information resource. Establish early on that you have researched their industry and their company and you know much more than only your business or service. You want to impress upon as many people as possible that you are the "go-to" person on long term care issues. Believe me, the referrals will follow.

3. You want your referral source to know the answer to their question, "Why?"

Especially *why* they should refer to you. *Why* you are the best resource for long term care. *Why* you can help them perform their jobs better.

You need to have a plan *before* setting the date for the presentation. Think about what the attendees want to hear and then decide how you want to present it.

Your emphasis should be on the benefits to *them*.

Setting the Appointment

In today's world of cut-backs, short staffing and mounds of paperwork for healthcare professionals, few have time to stop and listen to marketers just talk about their business. They do however have to eat. And everyone loves a free meal. This is why the Lunch & Learn is such a great marketing tool.

So how do you get in? Here are three basic approaches you could try:

1. Direct call. This works best because the results are instantaneous *and* it's an opportunity to begin a new relationship or strengthen an existing one. Call the secretary or administrative assistant and ask to be put on the schedule. Get to know this person well. He or she is the key to your future relations with this company.

2. Personal visit. This is a great method if you are good at forming relationships quickly, or if you already have an existing relationship or referral program in place. Bring an interesting item with you (candy jar, date pad, etc.) and ask if there are any available dates on the schedule. One advantage is that you will probably get to see where you will be presenting. This will help you decide how you will set up the room.

3. Deliver an invitation and follow-up with a phone call. This method combines the best of the other two. It involves hand delivering an invitation to the office of your prospective referral with recommended dates. This is a five-day process:

a) Send the invite.

b) Follow up with a personal call on the third day. The best part of this option is that you get to have fun. Send along some menu choices, your business cards and brochures, any other creative items that will impress them.

c) On day four, stop by with the invitation you have mailed in hand. This is a reminder and more impactful and also gives you a reason to re-visit.

d) Confirm your results on day five.

e) Provide a menu if possible. If you simply ask what they prefer, your budget may not be healthy enough for lobster.

If you're going to use this approach, be creative. Your envelope needs to scream *FREE LUNCH*!

No matter what method you use, be sure to send a confirmation of the meeting date, time, specifics, etc. This can even be in the form of a thank you note. If someone was instrumental in helping you get the appointment such as a secretary, receptionist, etc., send that person an individual thank you note as well.

It's not unusual for these dates to be several weeks or even months ahead of time. Calendars fill up quickly! Keeping this type of event as part of your annual marketing plan is just smart business. So, what are you waiting for?

QUICK TIP: Consider partnering with a complimentary service (e.g., assisted living and hospice, homecare and elder law, nursing homes and rehabilitation centers, etc.). This could save you time and money by splitting up the presentation and food preparation. This could also be another "in" for you if your partner has a mailing list, as well as a great networking relationship builder. You set the date and invite the other guy to join you.

A Word about Emails

You probably send and receive emails all day. However, in referral-based marketing, this type of relationship must be earned. You know how much SPAM and unsolicited emails you get. The delete button is probably the most used on your keyboard. Before you start using emails to communicate with a referral source, make sure that you have a relationship that supports it. You should both agree that this is a good method of communication between you. That way, when they see your name in the email address, they won't reach for the delete button right away.

Presentation Tactics

Every presentation is unique. Like the cover letter which accompanies your resume it should be specific to the group you are presenting to. One size fits all never does. These events can involve as few as three people to as many as 30 or more. Know as much about your audience ahead of time as you can.

The room is also a major factor. Anywhere from a small kitchen to a conference room could be used. Do your homework! The following are guidelines for each size group to make sure that you are remembered for a positive event. Should you be formal or create a relaxed atmosphere? Both! Of course, you will always be professional and make sure everyone is comfortable.

Here are some tips for different situations to help you craft your presentation.

If your audience is new and unfamiliar with your services...

Introduce and explain your services. Without egotism, demonstrate your and your company's knowledge of senior care and how your business addresses the needs of the elder population and caregivers. Ask them about their clientele and their experience with referrals to your type of facility. Invite them to come and personally see your facility.

If your audience is familiar with your services and has referred already...

Ask about their satisfaction with your services. Don't get defensive if you don't hear what you want to hear. This is an opportunity to discuss improvements that can be made. After—and only after—a discussion like this, talk about any new programs at your facility. If you have a story about any individual that they referred, this is a good time to use it.

In both instances, your goal is to build a strong relationship or strengthen an existing one. Remember, people like to work with people they like. Where have you heard that before?!

Some tips about presentation formats for different size audiences

Three or fewer attendees...

This is an intimate and sometimes too close for comfort setting. It will probably be held in a kitchenette, or someone's office or small conference room.

Introduce yourself if necessary and break the ice with small talk about their professions or the healthcare industry in general. There's always something to talk about in healthcare!

Keep the setting informal. Focus on one-on-one relationship building discussions, even if they are not necessarily work related.

Discuss the progress of their current referred residents. Update them with some stories of outstanding rehab results. Ask for ways to improve your service to them.

People like to talk about their jobs. Let them do the talking while you listen attentively. A good rule of thumb: *If you want to impress someone, be impressed by them.*

Four to 10 attendees...

This can be a comfortable but sometimes awkward format, depending on which players are in the room.

Start by presenting a question about healthcare such as, "There are so many options available today for our seniors—even some that I was not aware of. To start off, I'd like to share those with you today."

Open-ended, but it will get everyone thinking. Next you can tactfully discuss the specific option your company offers. Ask your audience to tell you about their practice and needs. Ask for ways to improve the service of senior care in general, etc. Focus on areas of interest specific to this group (e.g., rehab issues, orthopedics, etc.).

Keep the setting semi-informal. Be sure to talk to the entire group. Make eye contact with everyone and don't alienate any individual. Focus on group relationship-building discussions. Use your own personality to "work" the room.

Groups of 10 or larger

Be professional but not stuffy. This is an opportunity for you to show off your knowledge of the industry as it relates specifically to their patients. For example, if you are Memory Care, discuss specifics and how your facility meets those needs. Talk about alliances you already have with organizations, such as the Alzheimer Association, Hospital Pulmonary Units, etc.

Use a somewhat formal presentation style. *Educate*. Pick a topic and focus on facility relationship-building.

Keep your presentation interactive by asking lots of questions.

For this size group, it's a good idea to include your Administrator and/or Clinical Director and Therapy Manager for added impact.

Ideas for topics

• Veteran's Administration Allocation for helping veterans pay for assisted living, skilled nursing, etc.

• Special units in your facility (Pulmonary, Rehabilitation, Secured Units, etc.)

• Open discussion regarding types of insurance, organizations, etc.

• How can we fix that problem we had last week [month, etc.] so it doesn't happen again?

• Relevant issues with healthcare support services

If you have a good sense of humor, use it! If not, bring chocolate! It's OK to stray from the agenda. Talk about yourself and your family. Even better, get them to talk about themselves. Talk about your upcoming wedding, your history, their history, or their kids. Say something memorable. You want them to remember you for all the right reasons. Even if it's for your quirks. Remember, the goal is to build relationships. Keep the tone upbeat!

Preparation: Three Days Out

You've made the appointment, and everything is set. At least three days out, you should confirm all the details. Things change all the time in this business. Call the referral source and make sure that everything is still on for the scheduled date and time. Re-confirm the number of attendees and details. Make sure the room size is the same as originally discussed. Also, for small groups, make sure that nobody has any allergies to certain foods. Sound excessive? Imagine showing up with food that no one can eat. You can cater the type of meal to the audience by simply asking, "What kind of food do they like—a heavy lunch like pasta or pizza? Or lighter meals such as salads?" You can't please everyone but you can focus on the majority.

To be really creative and proactive, send a flyer to the site at least one week out as a reminder. This creates a bit of excitement and lets people know that they don't need to bring a lunch that day.

Make sure that you order the lunch three days out. If you are picking it up from a restaurant, let them know what time you will be there so that they have everything ready. You don't want any surprises on the day.

Rehearse! Rehearse! Rehearse! Whether you've been through the same presentation once or 10 times before, make sure you take the time to go over it again, with this specific audience in mind. This is especially important if you are presenting with a colleague or someone from a complimentary business. Take the time to rehearse together.

Luncheon checklist

Don't assume that the office or company where you are holding your presentation has anything. I've witnessed lunches without utensils, cups, plates, napkins, or ice. Be prepared and bring everything with you. Below is a checklist of all the items that you should have ready. Avoid last minute crises by having this all written down.

Details:

✓ Referral Name/Company:

✓ Contact Person and Phone Number:

✓ Luncheon Date/Time:

✓ Facility Address and Phone Number:

✓ Number of Attendees (include names if it's a small group):

✓ Subject of Presentation:

✓ Enough Leave Behind Material: Brochures, business cards, pens, information folder, cups, etc.

Other:

Food:

✓ Main Course (pasta, salad, sandwiches, pizza, etc.)

✓ Side Course (potato chips, potato salad, rolls and butter, etc.)

✓ Beverages (soda, iced tea, coffee, etc.) plus ice

✓ Dessert (cookies, pie, Danish, fruit, etc.)

✓ Always best to provide choices!

Utensils:

✓ Plastic forks, spoons, knives

✓ Plastic cups

✓ Plastic or paper plates

✓ Paper napkins

✓ Serving spatulas, knives, and spoons

Paper items are not as good for messy foods, but some companies are sensitive to non-environmentally friendly materials like plastics. Know your audience!

Meeting/Luncheon Day

Today's the day. And yes, this is a *presentation*. Everything you do in marketing from Lunch & Learns to one-on-one conversations is a presentation if you are talking about your business or service. You've done all the planning, phone calls, rehearsing and promotion. Now you need to pull it all together.

The following is a must-do checklist to follow today:

1) Arrive at least 20 to 30 minutes ahead to set up and acclimate yourself to the room. This allows plenty of time for deciding where to put out the food and drink, and where you will sit or stand for the presentation. This will make a big difference in your comfort level.

2) Set up the dining stations as quickly as possible. If you've done your homework, you have everything you need for the correct number of people. Distribute utensils, cups, napkins and any collateral materials or gifts you plan to provide. Next, set up the buffet-style food for ease of access.

3) As attendees begin to enter the room, stand tall and look professional. Introduce yourself to each individual as he or she arrives, and thank them all for attending. Ask them to help themselves in the food line. Smile throughout the entire process. Remember, these are the people you want to build relationships with. Use this time to assess your audience so you can make any last minute changes in your

presentation format. This is why it is important to be flexible. You never know for sure what will work until you meet them on the day.

4) Once all are seated with their meals, spend time socializing with those seated around you. It's OK to pre-present a bit to a few of them prior to getting started with the whole group. This will help you gain some confidence. It's also a good time to ask questions.

5) Don't wait for everyone to complete their meals before getting started. They're hungry, but they're busy too. Introduce yourself and your company to the group as a whole. Thank them for taking time out of their busy schedules to join you for lunch.

6) Be brief but informative. In this day of information overload, it's easy to overwhelm people with too much data. This is your opportunity to build relationships. You can use this forum to relate stories of residents they've referred, talk about industry issues, etc. Let the audience know what a valuable resource you are and how you can help them.

7) Always be cognizant of your timing. These are busy people and may not have much time. Keep your dialog to about 10 to 15 minutes overall. You can get more "face time" after your presentation with those who remain in the room. Be available for questions. For small groups this can be conversational.

8) Summarize. Make sure that everyone who attends knows why they were there and what you have to offer them. Be memorable. They might not go out humming the tune, but

they should feel as though they have received some kind of personal benefit in return for their time and attention.

Follow-Up

The most common form of marketing fall-out is marketing follow-up. If you've just met a group of people and conducted a successful Lunch & Learn, it's important to take it to the next level. Build on the relationships that have been started. Send thank you notes to the appropriate personnel who helped you get the meeting organized as well as key attendees. Ideally, they were all key attendees! If it was a small group, be sure to mention something specific to each one, referring back to the conversation you had. Schedule a follow-up meeting with anyone who you've got an "in" with from the luncheon.

Depending on the relationship you have, you could follow up by email. But hand written notes are much more personal and they get noticed (and very often, posted on the bulletin board in the office) so they help build relationships.

It's easy to forget names and faces, particularly in a large group. Be sure to keep a good record of the event:

- Name of attendee

- Title

- Pertinent info you picked up, such as connections, likes or dislikes, etc.:

You can create your own system using index cards, Excel spreadsheets or some of the many apps available on your iPhone.

If you're really serious about your career, subscribe to one of the services available.

Remember, the point of the Lunch & Learn is to create new relationships or build on existing ones. Approximately 20% of healthcare personnel change jobs every year. So everyone you have met is significant. They could show up in another company tomorrow.

CHAPTER SIX:

On Questions, Discussion and Dialog

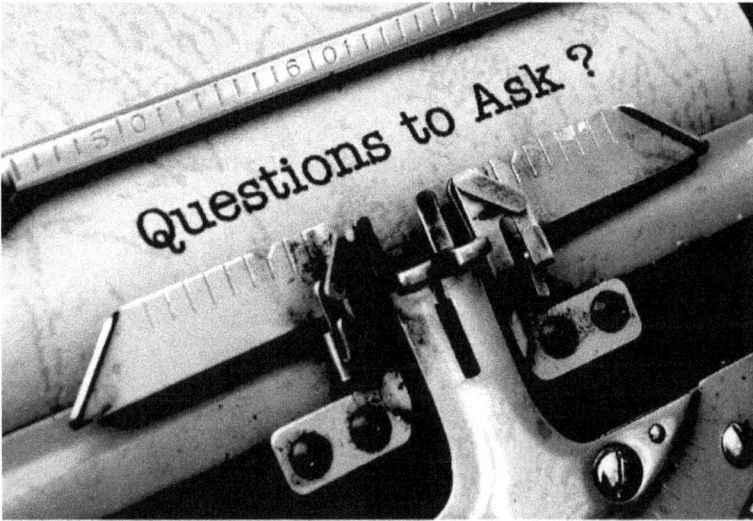

QUESTION: *"What is the process when you first meet with a marketer?"*

You got the appointment. You have anywhere from two to five minutes to start or build upon a relationship with a key referral source. What should you do? What have you done in the past? What works and what doesn't? What separates the good marketers from the great marketers? What do the doctors suggest?

RESPONSE #1:
"I can always tell if someone did his or her research. Asking appropriate questions is fine, but be careful not to turn it into an interrogation."

Starting off by asking questions about the types of insurance they work with and their typical patient count can come off as an interrogation. You should know what to begin with from your initial research with their staff or administrative assistants. Be conversational. There's an old adage that if you want to impress someone, be impressed by them. Find that connection—that's your initial topic.

If you already service any of this physician's patients, you can start by giving an update or status on them. If not, talk about the service you can provide in a conversational manner.

RESPONSE #2:
"Don't be pushy! Don't talk at me. Talk with me."

Nobody likes a pushy sales person. Building relationships should not be a pushy process. We've all had the experience of someone talking "at" us and we know how uncomfortable it can be. Talking to someone is a give-and-take situation and not one-sided. One physician emphasized: "Slow down!"

Be personable. Be yourself. After all—it's you that you're selling. Let them get to know you as you are getting to know them.

RESPONSE #3:

"It's important to me to know that the marketer and his or her company are patient-focused. Don't be all about your company."

Your delivery and presentation is important. Be sincere. It's difficult to fake sincerity. Your company hired you and your goal is to have your referral source "hire" you as well. If you're a nurse, elaborate on your expertise of understanding patient challenges. Show the doctor that you understand the need for each level of care and ALWAYS acknowledge the physician's expertise—never challenge their diagnosis. Offer information that may help, but don't take over as the clinical expert.

BONUS QUESTION:

"How do you feel about the direct approach of asking you for the referral?"

There is a lot of pressure from companies to have their marketers simply ask for the referral. As one salesperson put it, "They know I'm not here to collect their laundry." You are trying to build a relationship. However, there are times when your visit is short—especially if you already have the relationship—and a direct approach can be warranted. The responses to this question may surprise you.

Summarized responses to this question:
"I respect that. Few actually do it. I do like to know why I should use you over the competitor. What makes you stand out? How are you going to make it easy to work with you?"

Good marketers know how to ask without being intrusive, especially if you already have a working relationship together. Personally, I have used the direct approach of asking for the referral at the appropriate time. It's all about timing. Your instinct will tell you when that time arrives.

The relationship is still the key here. If you have a great relationship, you'll never have to ask for the referral.

The Prescription

Patient Name:_____
Address:_____ Date:_____

R℞

**SCRIPT ONE:
Be careful in
your approach.
Don't
interrogate!**

MD:_____
Signature:_____

Be conversational and don't sound like a hard-sell salesperson. Remember, you're selling yourself, not the company or service.

Patient Name:_____
Address:_____ Date:_____

R℞

**SCRIPT TWO:
Provide
credibility to
your company's
service record.**

MD:_____
Signature:_____

Provide credibility through testimonials or reference. If you are currently servicing a patient of the physician or a resident from the facility, provide an update or explain how the family/patient is supportive of your services.

Patient Name:_____
Address:_____ Date:_____

R℞

SCRIPT THREE: Don't be afraid to ask for the referral.

MD:_____
Signature:_____

It's all a matter of timing. Trust your instinct to know when the time is right. A good guideline is that it is usually better to ask for the referral during the conversation, at the beginning or middle, rather than at the end as an afterthought. Once you have developed a strong working relationship, you won't have to ask.

CHAPTER SEVEN:

On Communication and Follow-Up

QUESTION: *"How important is communication between you and your marketer following a referral?"*

People may doubt what you say, but they will believe what you do. – Lewis Cass, 22nd U.S. Secretary of State.

The number one reason that most referral connections fail is the lack of follow-up after the initial meeting. Out of sight, out of mind! Lack of follow-up sends a message. It shows a lack of interest. If you don't plan on committing to this relationship with a strong focus, don't start it at all.

Communication is a skill to be learned and mastered. Everyone sends and receives messages in a different way. Understanding the expectations of your referral source will help. Once a referral has been made, poor communication can not only damage the relationship but also send a negative message about your company or service.

RESPONSE #1:
"Follow-up is one of the most important parts of this process, especially with my office and support staff. Also, be honest if something goes wrong. Things happen."

The marketing process doesn't stop with the initial referral. Whether it's a physician, a discharge planner, or an administrator of a long-term care facility, your referral source will want to know that they have received the best care possible.

Once a referral is made, you become an important part of the referral source's staff as the patient's care continues. The communication expectations of the physician or referring individual are your concern. Too much or too little communication can only be determined by that individual so it's important to discuss upfront the desired method of communication (phone, email, texting, personal visit, personal meetings, etc.).

Healthcare marketing is about identifying the right person to communicate with and the right approach. Your initial connection may start with the physician but the majority of the communication may be through the physician's assistant or a designated office professional (scheduler, discharge planner, etc.). Once you identify that person, determine the right type of communication to use. This

WHAT THE DOCTOR ORDERS

could be phone call, text message, email or fax. During your research, find out how the office communicates with other resources as well. This will help you with your process.

Let me explain with a personal example.

When I was an administrator, one of my residents was referred to a hospice company. This required a physician's signature which our nursing director helped to expedite. During the course of the care, the hospice sent the resident to the hospital where he remained for about two weeks.

The communication between the facility and the hospice was thorough. What did not happen, however, was communication with the resident's physician. Only when making his rounds at the facility was the physician notified that the resident had been admitted to the hospital—10 days earlier. No one took the time to communicate this information to the physician's office. Which individual was at fault? Does it really matter?

The physician's communication with the family was jeopardized as was the facility and the hospice's relationship with the physician. It took almost one year to rebuild those relationships. It all could have been avoided by simply following up with the original source, the physician.

RESPONSE #2:
"Again, the relationship is key. Turnover is terrible. I just start to get used to someone and then they're gone. I refer to people not companies."

The relationships you form are part of your personal reputation. Many of the physicians agreed that, if a

87

marketer whom they had a good relationship with moved on to another company, they would follow him or her. This underlines the importance of developing a personal brand. You want to be known for providing great service and your staff is a reflection of your brand.

Create a profile for each referral source. If you move onto another job by choice, you should pass this information onto your replacement. This becomes part of your personal brand. There is a sample profile form in Appendix B.

RESPONSE #3:
"Sometimes I have a problem when I meet and trust the marketer. But then the staff their company sends to provide the service is less than adequate and I can't reach the marketer to discuss the issue."

It still surprises me that some companies will spend good money on excellent marketers and then hire the equivalent of a Rottweiler to work the front desk or take phone calls.

This book is full of tactics and ideas to get referrals from healthcare sources, but you also need to be familiar with the staff you are sending in to actually perform the service. Many business relationships have been derailed as a result of poor service delivered after a marketer secured the original relationship.

The best way to monitor this is to make sure that you are available to accompany the staff on that first visit to the facility or patient to make the proper introductions. Marketing schedules are tight, and this may not always be possible. Make sure you at least follow up within a few days after the first service visit to ensure that your referral is pleased with the service.

RESPONSE #4:
"Trust is one of the most important characteristics I look for. This is all part of making it easy to work with you."

A give-and-take communication process is a strong indication of trust between the parties. Miscommunication, missed diagnoses, missed phone calls, and a variety of other unfortunate occurrences can happen. When something does go wrong, be honest. All of the respondents to these interviews offered related stories of this kind. And each agreed that when notified as soon as there was a problem, they were able to solve it together.

It's not the size nor the scope of the challenge; it's how you handle it that builds on the relationship.

RESPONSE #5:
"Do what you say you're going to do and communicate that you did it. This is important. I hate surprises."
(NHA/PCHA)

The only thing worse than not following up is not following through. Our industry is a fast-moving business, similar to the field of advertising which I used to work in. But healthcare involves lives. The timing of the care being provided, the processing of the paperwork, dotting the i's and crossing the t's to keep everything moving quickly and according to regulations and rules is important. And this may also be the most important part of the process for you as a marketer since most errors tend to happen here.

The respondents to this question were all the same. Follow through on the entire process. And if there's a change—for example, if a discharge date from the hospital is altered due to health conditions—make sure you notify all of the relevant stakeholders.

In many cases a referral requires changes in staffing, rooms, medication preparation, and scheduling, as well as tons of paperwork. Sometimes insurance companies extend hospital stay; a patient's health status changes, transportation issues force schedule conflicts. You need to be on top of the process early in the business partnership, when it is the most volatile. Whatever happens will always come back to the marketer—*you*!

BONUS QUESTION:

"Do any of the marketers refer to you? Do they help you (or your team) to network? Is this important to you?"

While very few of the physicians I interviewed had much to say about this due to their already large clientele, the nursing home and assisted living administrators were quick to provide their input.

RESPONSES:

"I am ultimately responsible for the entire operation which includes census growth. If I am using a hospice, homecare or rehab service in my facility, I have an expectation that those marketers will refer and help me build my numbers." *(NHA/PCHA)*

"Those companies that refer to me are the companies I want to build a strong, lasting relationship with." *(NHA/PCHA)*

Although the final decision is always up to the resident or family when choosing a resource of care, as an administrator I was able to present the family with options. In addition to making sure that the care of my resident would be exemplary, I would always provide include those companies that referred to my facility at the top of the list.

It's simple math. If you are going to market to a facility, be ready and open to marketing that facility to your clientele. Hospice and homecare professionals provide many services to patients who are still in their own home. Part of that service is making sure that their needs are covered. They are also the first to notice that the individual can no longer live on their own. This is how you refer to facilities. And this is also how you build a strong, trusting relationship with those professionals. A physician or long-term care facility will always refer and provide access to any healthcare company that helps them build their business through mutual referrals.

I also strongly encourage the marketer of those services to be involved with the care monitoring. Your credibility as a marketer is based on the delivery of service by your care staff. One administrator told me that when something goes awry, she calls the marketer, not the clinical staff. I agree with this technique. After all, you, the marketer, sold me the service.

The Prescription

Patient Name:_____
Address:_____ Date:_____

R℞

**SCRIPT ONE:
Follow-up is your
most important
tool in building
relationships.**

MD:_____
Signature:_____

It's also a great way to say thank you and provide resource information at the same time. A follow-up can also be your opportunity to re-visit the office and strengthen your relationship.

Patient Name:_____
Address:_____ Date:_____

R℞

SCRIPT TWO:
It's your
reputation.

MD:_____
Signature:_____

Because referrals are ultimately based on the strength of the relationship, it's all about your processing and servicing of the account at all levels. Make sure you know your team and clinical supervisors who are delivering on your promise of great service.

Patient Name:_____
Address:_____ Date:_____

R℞

SCRIPT
THREE:
Follow-up is
useless without
follow-through.

MD:_____
Signature:_____

Acquiring the referral is only the first step of the entire process. Making sure that everything runs smoothly is what keeps the relationship strong and the referrals coming.

Patient Name:_____
Address:_____ Date:_____

R̽

**SCRIPT FOUR:
Provide referrals
to your clientele
to help them grow
their business as
well as your own.**

MD:_____
Signature:_____

The purpose of every business is to grow their census or patient base. If you receive a referral make it a point to provide in return. Also, be involved in the care to maintain a good reputation and future business.

Chapter Eight:

Special Bonus Section

Ideas for Marketing to Professionals

Professional referrals are the heartbeat of the long-term care business. Why? Because for the most part, no one in their 60s, 70s or 80s is going to walk into your facility (Skilled Nursing, Personal Care or Assisted Living) and ask to move in! The same goes for hospice and home care – your clients or patients won't call you on the phone and ask to stop by. Of course there are the all-important calls from family members, but the majority of inquiries come from your professional referral sources.

In addition to the physicians interviewed for this book, the following is a list of the most common referral sources for long-term care marketers:

Adult Daycare

Alzheimer Association

Assisted Living Facilities (for Skilled Nursing)

Discharge Planners

Home Health Agencies

Hospice Services

Hospitals

Independent Living

Outpatient Clinics

Placement Agencies

Private Nursing Services (for Assisted Living Facilities)

Rehabilitation Centers

Senior Centers

Skilled Nursing Centers

Social Services

Attitude, service and relationships are the key aspects of any healthcare marketing director's program. As has been stressed often in this book – people like to work with people they like. If you build great relationships you will insure a continual stream of referrals to maintain census growth.

In this section you'll find ideas focusing on building and retaining relationships with the professional referral audience, making good use of healthcare observances and recognition events. I've listed some of the most common occurrences and provided you with a couple of quick ideas to help with your planning.

Great marketing requires creative thinking. Brainstorming requires that you think in the "opposite" direction of your intended goal. For example, instead of calling your referral sources, why not have them call you? Below I offer two quick ideas that you can use any day of the year to give your referral source a reason to get in touch!

The "Law of Reciprocity" says that when you do something to make other people feel good, they unconsciously want to return the favor. Below, "Many Happy Returns" provides you with an open door invitation with your referral source to periodically stop by.

Healthcare marketing budgets tends to be small. Low costs and high impact are the answer. These professional referral ideas will put you ahead in the game of building census.

REASONS TO CALL

A Reason to Call #1: *It's a Starbucks Morning*

Everybody loves to start their day off with coffee. Especially if someone else will stop by a coffee specialty shop and buy it for them.

Strategy: Rewards and thanks current referral sources and gently reminds them to refer to you.

Objective: Keeps you (and your residence) top of mind and gets the referral source to contact you. Great relationship builder (and conversation piece)!

Process: Send or fax an "Invitation/Announcement" and beverage menu from a local specialty coffee shop (e.g.,

Starbucks, Seattle's Best, etc.) to current referral sources approximately seven days prior to event. List names of recipients (discharge planner, social worker, etc.) with a request for response. At five days out, send a reminder fax. If all orders have been received, send an "excitement" reminder two days out.

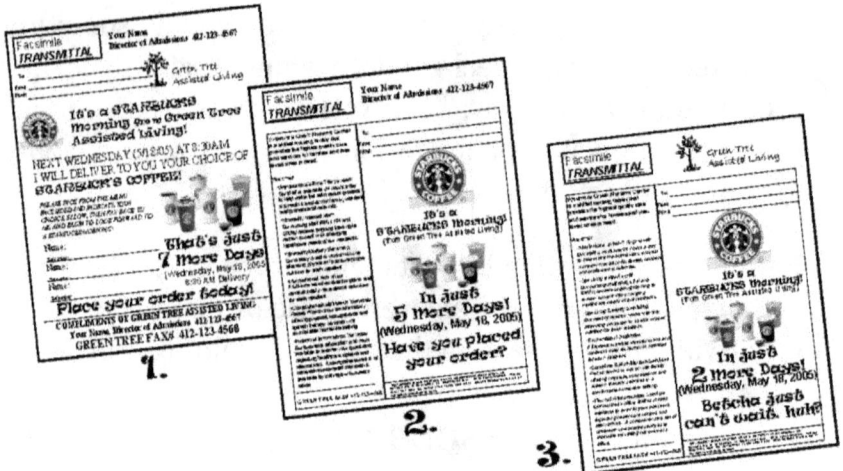

Elements:

- Fax Invitation Sheet
- Menu Fax Reminder
- Excitement Sheet
- Nearby specialty coffee shop

Cost: Depends on the number of referral sources at each hospital, rehab, etc. (average $20 to $30). (If it's a large order, they might even give you a quantity discount!)

A Reason to Call #2: *The Breakfast Card Club*

Providing bagels and cream cheese or pastries has been an overused marketing tactic for years. In this case, you turn the process into a reward and a thank you for referrals received. Same concept. Different message.

Strategy: Rewards and thanks current referral sources and gently reminds them to refer to you.

Objective: Keeps you (and your residence) top of mind and gets the referral source to call you to implement. Great relationship builder (and conversation piece)! Your referral source will contact YOU!

Process: Write a thank you letter on company letterhead and include a Breakfast Ticket--a laminated card with your logo on it. Mail to key referral individual (head discharge planner, etc.).Call in a few days to confirm delivery--although, in most cases they will call you and implement quickly. When they get in touch, take bagels to the referral source and pick up the ticket (for reuse). Repeat in 4 to 6 weeks.

Special Recognition and Thank You!

Your Facility LOGO

Breakfast CARD

This Coupon Good for 1 'Baker's Dozen'

BAGELS AND CREAM CHEESE

Simply call your FACILITY NAME'S Admissions Director, YOUR NAME at 000-000-0000 at least 24 hours prior to delivery and you will receive 13 fresh bagels and 2 cream cheese (1 regular and 1 flavored) delivered to your office by 8:45AM the next morning.

YOUR NAME, Admissions Director   000-000-0000

Courtesy of **YOUR FACILITY** of YOUR CITY

TICKET CK15-0305

Elements:

- Thank you/recognition letter on company letterhead signed by you (and your administrator).

- Breakfast Card printed on fluorescent paper, laminated, if possible, for re-use.

Cost: Average $25/$30 for bagels and cream cheese or pastries. Once again, ask for a quantity discount!

MANY HAPPY RETURNS

Many Happy Returns #1: *The Re-Fillable Candy Jar*

It's gotten a bit more difficult to provide gifts to your referral sources. This is especially true when it comes to larger companies such as hospitals or rehabilitation centers. I still believe that a strong relationship with a referral source can get around restrictive policies.

Strategy: Keep your name and facility name top-of-mind in their offices. Provides the opportunity to re-fill the container as needed (at least once per month).

Objective: Great relationship retainer program (and conversation piece)! Doesn't require face-to-face meeting; works daily to keep your name (and facility) top-of-mind.

Process: Purchase container, preferably a glass jar or other decorative container, with your facility's name, logo AND phone number imprinted on it. Deliver and place in your referral's office in easy view of all staff. Visit frequently and re-fill.

Bonus tip: Ahead of time, ask people in the office to tell you their favorite candy—M&Ms, Skittles, Gum, Hershey Chocolate, etc. DON'T BE CHEAP!

Elements:

- Customized container or glass jar.

- Candy, bubblegum, mints, etc. depending on the office preference.

Cost: Low: Average $10 to $15 for container and candy.

Another bonus tip: This program requires consistent monitoring; if you're going to do it, do it right! Nothing is worse than dead plants, dusty plants, outdated themes—or an empty candy jar.

Many Happy Returns #2: *The Seasonal Flower Arrangement*

Everybody loves to create an ambiance in their workspace. Flowers provide a nice addition to any office and in most cases would be openly welcome. Sometimes a logo on a vase may attract attention and cause issues, but your referral source will remember where they came from.

The Re-fillable* Seasonal Flower Arrangement!

Strategy: Keep your name and facility top-of-mind in their offices. Provides opportunity to re-fill container as needed (minimally once per month).

Objective: Great relationship retainer program (and conversation piece)! Doesn't require face-to-face meeting; works daily to keep your name (and facility) top-of-mind. Gives you a reason to come and visit your referral source.

Process: Purchase decorative vase with your facility's name, logo AND phone number imprinted. Deliver (and place) in your referral's work area (lunchroom, conference room, receptionist area, etc.) in clear view of all staff. Visit frequently and re-fill with current holiday's theme.

Elements:

- Customized vase.

- Flower arrangement, holiday themed items (flags, ribbons, etc.).

Cost: Low—Average $15 to $25 for vase and flower arrangement.

HEALTHCARE OBSERVANCES AND EVENTS

When you're marketing to referral sources and building relationships, it's always good to take advantage of national or local healthcare recognition days. Many of these dates may mean nothing to the consumer but to your audience, this may be the only recognition they get. Their jobs are often based heavily on the "labor of love" philosophy – modest income but high satisfaction of providing care for those who may have no one. The following is a list of the most common recognition days, but there are many more, including national holidays.

January

- Blood Donor Month

- Glaucoma Awareness Month (National)

- Intravenous Nurse Day (25th)

- Medical Group Practice Week (Last week)

The holidays are over. Throughout the year I've seen several blood drives held at facilities as well as community venues. This is a great opportunity to partner with one of your referral sources to hold such a drive. Additionally Glaucoma Awareness offers a great opportunity to provide audio books and conduct an educational session for one of your referral sources.

Intravenous Nurse Day is the perfect opportunity to market your services to dialysis clinics. Medical Group Practice Week offers thea chance to meet new physicians joining existing group practice teams in your market area.

February

- American Heart Month
- Patient Recognition Week (1st week)
- Pride in Food Service Week (2nd week)
- Cardiac Rehab Week (2nd week)
- Cardiovascular Professionals Week (3rd Week)

In addition to national holidays such as Valentine's Day, February is a key month to focus on all of your referral sources when it comes to cardiac. Taking collections for cardiac research in the name of your referral source is one option. Cardiac rehab week presents the opportunity to use the refillable candy promotion discussed earlier by delivering red wrapped chocolates, or heart healthy sweets

Targeting cardiovascular professionals at the hospitals or group practices and tying your promotions in with the heart theme to recognize them is paramount.

Pride in Food Service Week is a chance to present healthy eating habits to staff. Any lunch meetings should highlight the benefits of organic foods and lifestyle changes.

March

- American Red Cross Month
- National Social Worker Month
- Pulmonary Rehabilitation Week (2nd week)
- American Diabetes Alert Day (4th Tuesday)
- National Physician's Day (30th)

While all of the above listed holidays offer great opportunities for your marketing, the two most important are Social Worker month, which is a key target for any healthcare marketer, and Physicians Day.

The following promotion ideas have worked for me in the past and I highly recommend them.

1. National Social Worker's Month

Ode to a Social Worker

Social workers not only work closely with physicians, discharge planners, and all types of healthcare professionals, they also work directly with families in crisis. This makes them one of the most important referral sources you can target and one of the least recognized.

Strategy: Recognition of Social Workers and the contributions they make to the LTC industry. A great opportunity to thank them for their services to you and your marketing efforts.

Timing: March is National Social Workers' Month Also works for special recognition of outstanding service.

Objective: Recognizes one of the most important individuals in the admissions and marketing process. By personalizing a plaque with the following poem or one that you create yourself, you are single-handedly showing how much you appreciate the social worker's importance.

Process: Have a professional plaque produced at a local trophy shop. Provide them with the poem on parchment paper as shown. Present to Social Worker at formal function or hand deliver and present with hospital senior manage-ment in attendance.

Cost: Depending on the quality and engraving costs, average $40 to $60 for each hospital.

Social
Worker
Month

Presented to

**HOSPITAL NAME
AND LOGO**

by

**YOUR COMPANY
NAME AND LOGO**

Ode to a Great
Social Worker!

You are a patient advocate,
Listener
and friend…
A community resource
provider,
The list doesn't end!

You are a counselor,
Educator
A discharge planner too…
A mediator,
You are always learning
something new!

You are a care plan decision
maker,
Admission planner
A resource for staff…
Knowledgeable about the
latest regulations,
You wear many hats!

In recognition of National
Social Work Month
And all that you do…
We wanted to say, "Thank
you!"
We sure appreciate you!

2. National Physician's Day

Specialized Physician Gifts

As mentioned throughout this book, it's important to truly know everything you can about the physician referral source. Using all that knowledge, March 30 is an important day for you to strengthen that relationship. This is your opportunity to stand out.

Strategy: Thank referring physicians by offering special gifts tailored to each physician's interests. Builds relationships with attending physicians and results in increased referrals.

Timing: National Doctor's Day in March, also physician birthdays, holidays or special thank you for specific deed.

Objective: Shows physicians that you took the time to find out about them. Gifts stand out instead of just being lumped in with the multitudes of gifts received from competitors.

Process: By contacting the nurses, receptionist, office personnel, etc. at your referring physicians.

Ideas: Imported wine, wine glasses, theme ties, special cigars, audio books, articles of clothing, CD Players, Sushi Machine (yes, I'm serious), customized smoking pipes, etc.

Cost: Could be expensive but worth the expense because the physician has major clout in referrals. Average $30 to $60 depending on the item.

Caution: 1. Make sure you check with the staff first to make sure that the doctor drinks wine, and 2. Don't be so generous that it would be seen as a bribe, by the physician or the organization's policy.

April

- National Occupational Therapy Month
- Hospital Admitting Clerks Day (1st —yes, really)
- National Public Health Week (1st Full Week)
- Patient Advocacy Week (2nd Week)
- Administrative Professionals Day (3rd Wednesday)
- National Volunteer Week (3rd full week)

The hospital admitting clerks may be a direct link to helping you get past the gatekeeper and I guarantee you that almost nobody gives them any recognition. The fact that it's also April Fools' Day should give you a great deal of creative ideas.

The opportunity to pamper administrative assistants on Professionals Day is a gift to them, and to their administrator. Having them come to your facility where you can provide massages, a light breakfast or salad lunch along with hiring a speaker or comedian for their enjoyment would be a great stress release. They would also remember you when you try to get into their facilities to see their leaders.

May

- National High Blood Pressure Month
- Older Americans Month
- National Nurses Week (always the 6th to the 12th)
- Nursing Home Week (2nd full week)
- National Hospital Week (2nd full week)
- National Women's Health Week (2nd full week)
- National Emergency Medical Services Week (3rd week)
- Older Americans' Mental Health Week (4th Sunday or last full week)
- National Senior Health & Fitness Day (always the last Wednesday)

Taking blood pressures as part of National High Blood Pressure Month may seem over-done, but combining it with an educational presentation may present oppor-tunities for you to extend it to the community as well. If held at a local facility this may be considered a marketing event for both you (as a home care, hospice or rehab company) and the facility providing the venue.

Older Americans Month is also a great opportunity to provide entertainment or information to the residence and patients at some of your referral sources' facilities.

Nurses Week can be combined with Nursing Home Week since many skilled facilities employ a high number of nurses. A lunchtime presentation which includes a CEU certificate along with key promotional items such as coffee mugs, etc. is usually a welcome event.

National Hospital Week represents a great opportunity for you to provide raffle items or giveaways with your contact information enclosed.

Finally, National Emergency Medical Services Week is a great opportunity to pay homage and recognize a key referral source that we seldom think about. In many cases, these professionals are the first to see and acknowledge that an individual needs assistance. Be honest, have you ever marketed to an EMT?

June

- National Men's Health Week (2nd Monday)
- Career Nurse Assistants Day (2nd Thursday)
- Nursing Assistants Week (2nd Week)

Summertime has traditionally been a slow period for healthcare marketers. We've all focused on the administrator and the nurses in the facilities, but have you ever considered marketing to the CNAs?

The assistants in most cases provide the bulk of the care in our industry, are paid the least, and recognized very seldom unless the facility has a program in place. Consider doing something for them during the summer months. It will pay off in the long run.

July

- National Therapeutic Recreation Week (2nd Full Week)
- Everybody Deserves a Massage Week (3rd Week)
- Healthcare Hospitality Week (3rd Full Week)

The most interesting holiday in July (apart from Independence Day, of course) is *Everybody Deserves a Massage Week*. In an industry that is infamous for stress it would seem prudent as a marketer to schedule a traveling masseuse and schedule individual massages for your referral source. If you don't want to go that far, you can always purchase massage gift certificates and provide them to your referral source. Everyone deserves a massage—even physicians!

August

- National Health Center Week
- Cataract Awareness Month
- Health Unit Coordinator Day (23rd)

August is a great month to plan for the next quarter but don't forget to recognize coordinators at the hospitals. Health Center Week is a good opportunity to introduce yourself to the many health service clinics. Remember that most of them are connected in some way to the hospitals in the area.

September

- Healthy Aging Month

- National Food Safety Education Month

- International Housekeepers Week (2nd full week)

- Assisted Living/Personal Care Home Week (3rd Week)

- National Rehabilitation Week (3rd week)

- National Women's Health & Fitness Day (last Wednesday)

- Family Health & Fitness Days USA (Last Saturday)

Family Health & Fitness Days USA is a great opportunity to introduce yoga to your referral sources. Hire an instructor for your facility or provide free tickets to a Saturday morning event. This conveniently coincides with Healthy Aging Month.

Every hospital has a Rehabilitation unit. Stop by and surprise them with coffee or breakfast. They've got a long day ahead. A focus on women's health provides you with activities for the second health and fitness day.

Meditation is a great stress-reliever. There are numerous recordings of guided meditation on the Internet. Providing

CDs and videos to facilities would be a twist on healthy living that may be welcome.

October

- Alzheimer's Memory Walk Month
- American Heart Walk Month Healthy Choice
- Halloween Safety Month
- National Family Health Month
- National Physical Therapy Month
- Talk About Prescriptions Month
- Gerontology Nursing Week (1st Week)
- Care Management Week (2nd Week)
- Physician's Assistants Week (2nd Week)
- National Healthcare Quality Week (2nd full week)
- Medical Assistants' Week (3rd work week)
- National Pharmacy Week (3rd week)
- National Primary Care Week (3rd week)
- Respiratory Care Week (Last week)

Many walks and races are held during this period. This is an opportunity to supply promotional items such as coffee cups, hats and energy food bars with your logo and business card.

The entire month is also devoted to physical therapy. Many physical therapists are working on an outsourced capacity with personal care and assisted living homes. They provide a connection for you to meet some of their contacts. This is another key group to build a relationship with.

November

- American Diabetes Month
- COPD Awareness Month
- Family Caregiver Month
- National Alzheimer's Disease Awareness Month
- National Home Care Month
- National Hospice Month
- PH (Pulmonary Hypertension) Awareness Month
- National Allied Health Week (2nd full week)

Hospice is one of the most misunderstood services in the healthcare community. If you are a hospice marketer, this is a great opportunity to set the record straight. Conduct presentations and highlight some of the people who have used your services and are living comfortable lives

Information on preventable Alzheimer's and memory care diseases can be presented in community centers as well as physicians' offices.

December

- International Day of Persons with Disabilities (December 3rd)
- Holiday Time!

December is a month of giving back and gratefulness. You've worked with your referrals all year and now is the time to back off the aggressive marketing. While gifts are fine for referrals with whom you've crafted strong relationships, the following ideas send your message without you needing to be present.

PROFESSIONAL DROP-OFF IDEAS

Drop-Off Ideas #1: *The Holiday Cheese/Fruit Plate*

Strategy: Retain relationships with current referral sources by keeping your name and facility top-of-mind in their offices.

Timing: December, prior to Christmas, and/or New Year's Eve; Easter holiday as well. Also works for "Anytime" Thank You.

Objective: Great relationship retainer program (and conversation piece)! Doesn't require face-to-face meeting, only drop off with promotional brochure/flyer or holiday thank you card.

Process: Purchase cheese/fruit or have your dietary manager prepare a special arrangement, and deliver to your referrals' office prior to lunch or after 1:30 PM. Include a holiday card from you or your company with a thank you message. Great around holidays and special recognitions.

Elements:

- Cheese/fruit plate
- Holiday/Thank you card.

Cost: Medium: Average $25 to $30 for cheese plate.

Drop-Off Ideas #2: *The Holiday Cookie Plate*

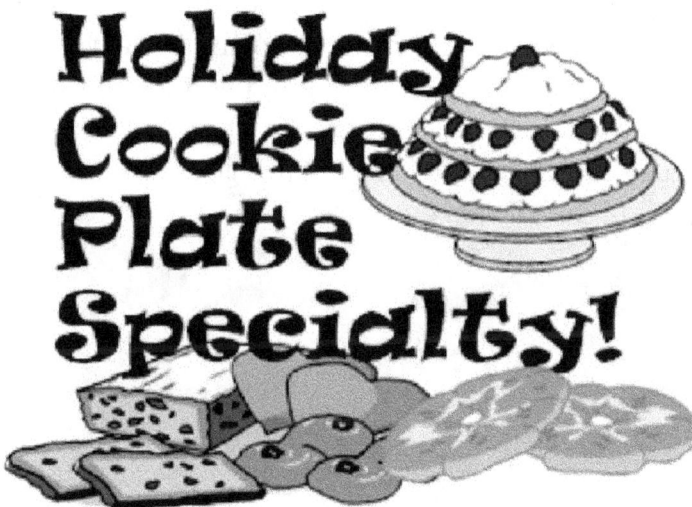

Timing: December, prior to Christmas, and/or New Year's Eve; Easter holiday as well. Also works for "Anytime" Thank You.

117

Strategy: Great relationship retainer program (and conversation piece)! Doesn't require face-to-face meeting; only drop off with promotional brochure, flyer or holiday thank you card.

Process: Purchase cookies/cakes, or have your dietary manager bake a special arrangement, and deliver to your referrals' office first thing in the morning. Great around holidays and special recognitions.

Elements:

- Cookies or cake
- Holiday/Thank you card.

Cost: Low: Average $15 to $20 for cookies.

It's important to remember to stand out in your marketing efforts and always look for the opportunity in every gesture. Even though this is a common practice for marketing during the holiday season, use brochures, business cards, and custom candy bars (with your logo) to promote and set yourself up for the next year.

SUMMARY AND PARTING THOUGHTS

In marketing, perception is reality. And as a marketing professional, you know more than you think you do. But it's easy to get caught up in the same old routine and fail to see the many opportunities to improve your game.

The bottom line in healthcare marketing is building a solid relationship with your referral source. This is done through strategic planning and timing. Researching your prospect and finding ways to make yourself a valued resource will put you at the top of your game. You are working with people who want to be served faster and better. They are looking for more information and a more efficient way of dealing with an increasingly procedure-laden process.

The skills necessary to excel as a marketer are learned-skills--in other words, you can become proficient through practice. Basic people skills combined with strong presentation techniques and detailed communication practices such as listening and asking the right questions are the most important tools you have.

We asked the questions and the answers are here for you to benefit from. I've provided you with my approach as well as some ideas you can try on your own. Be creative and keep up with the changes, understand your competition and anticipate the needs of the future marketplace—that is just what the doctor orders.

APPENDIX A:

Complete List of Interview Questions

A total of approximately 25 individuals participated in this survey (14 referring physicians, eight long-term care healthcare administrators, and three hospital discharge planners). The questions listed below are the ones which were used in the interview process. You could use them as discussion guides when you meet with any referral source, adapting them to your style and the person you're talking with.

1) How important is it for your marketer to REALLY know your business before they meet with you?

2) Can you tell if a marketer is green about their business or service?

3) Do you learn things from any of the marketers visiting you? Are any of them resources?

4) Do you find listening skills weak in marketers? Are they really listening to you or are they waiting to talk again?

5) Do they ask appropriate questions? What type of questions do you ask them?

6) Do any of the marketers refer to you? Do they help you (or your team) to network? Is this important to you?

7) How do you feel about marketers offering to educate your staff? Are you open to this?

8) What is the process of a typical marketing experience when they first meet with you?

9) Do you prefer the meeting to be patient-focused? How important is communication between you and your marketer following a referral from you?

10) How do you feel about relationships with your key referral resources? Is it important to you?

11) If possible for you to identify, what is the one thing that irritates you to the point of never referring to that marketer/company?

12) When you set a time to meet with a marketer, how much time do you typically allow? Five minutes? 10 minutes?

13) How do you feel about Lunch & Learn sessions at your office? How would you like them to proceed? Informational? Relationship-oriented?

14) In your office, who typically handles the referral process? Is it based on your input or theirs? Do you get involved at all in the process?

APPENDIX B:

Tools and samples
PHYSICIAN/REFERRAL PROFILE FORM

Every individual in a referral network should have a profile. The physician, administrator, discharge planner and, yes, even the administrative assistants attached to each referral–they know the rules and the details. This should be a one-page document. (see example on the following page). The document and its instructions are available at the link shown.

This document can be downloaded at
www.phdmkt.com/profile.

PHYSICIAN/REFERRAL PROFILE

Every individual in a referral network should have a profile. The physician, administrator, discharge planner and, yes, even the administrative assistants attached to each referral – they know the rules and the details. This should be a one-page document.

REFERRAL NAME: _____ PREFERENCES: _____

COMPANY/PRACTICE: _____

ADDRESS: _____ CITY: _____ STATE: _____ ZIP: _____

PHONE: _____ CELL: _____ FAX: _____ WEBSITE: _____

GENERAL INTERESTS: _____

SPECIFIC INTEREST (ACTOR, MUSICIAN, SPORTS, ETC) : _____

BEST VISIT TIMES/OFFICE HOURS: _____ MEMBER/ORGANIZATIONS: _____

PERSONALITY TRAITS: _____

PET PEEVES: _____

INSURANCE(S): _____ SPECIALTIES: _____

LEVEL-OF-RELATIONSHIP RATING (SCALE 1 – 10, 10 BEING SOLID RELATIONSHIP): _____ ACTIVE AS OF: _____ REFERRALS: Y   N

REFERRED BY (IF NOT COLD CALL) : _____ 1ST VISIT DATE/TIME: _____ RATING: _____

ADDITIONAL COMPANY INFORMATION:

ADMINISTRATIVE ASSISTANT: _____ RECEPTIONIST: _____

PERSONALITIES: _____

PET PEEVES: _____ LIKES: _____

LUNCH & LEARNS (Y/N), IF YES: DATE(S): _____ TOPICS: _____

FOOD PREFERENCES: _____ AVOID: _____

PHYSICIAN ASSISTANT/OFFICE MANAGER: _____

CLINICAL CONTACT (IF DIFFERENT FROM REFERRAL): _____

ISSUES WITH THIS REFERRAL (PAST OR PRESENT AND RESOLUTION): _____

_____

OPPORTUNITIES: _____

APPENDIX C:
Other books and resources

Although this book is largely based on a series of interviews with referring physicians, healthcare administrators and discharge planners, numerous books and resources have influenced my approach to marketing and leadership. You will find a few direct references to the following books. I have also included a few that offer valuable insight into relationship marketing.

<hr/>

Avrin, David. *It's Not Who You Know. It's Who Knows You!* Hoboken, NJ: John Wiley & Sons, Inc, 2010.

What are you doing to be seen and remembered? How are you ensuring your top-of-mind status with your referral sources? This book provides great insight into using the media and your personality to someone who people know can deliver.

Bacon, Terry R. *Elements of Influence: The Art of Getting Others to Follow Your Lead*. New York, NY: American Management Association, 2012.

Influence is a science. It is made up of the words you use, the body language you project, the way you dress, your tone of voice, etc. This book provides great insight into using the media and your personality to make yourself into someone who people know can deliver.

Covey, Stephen M.R. *The Speed of Trust: The One Thing That Changes Everything*. New York, NY: Simon & Shuster, Inc. 2006.

An often misused statement is, "It's who you know." This book sets the record straight and explains in great detail the importance of becoming a brand unto yourself. In health-care, people don't buy the facility or service—they buy based on their relationship with the seller, *you*.

Karten, Naomi. *Managing Expectations: Working with People Who Want More, Better, Faster, Sooner, NOW!* New York, NY: Dorset House Publishing, 1994.

This book is a crucial element in building relationships. Understanding the expectations of your referral source is the main element in "What the Doctor Orders" and this book discusses some of the most forgotten aspects of researching your source.

Maxwell, John C. *Everyone Communicates, Few Connect: What The Most Effective People Do Differently* Nashville, TN: Thomas Nelson, Inc, 2010.

John Maxwell is one of the top authors in the field of leadership and communication strategies. This book in particular is a gold mine of information on building strong relationships through common "talk" strategies.

━━◦◦◦◦◦◦━━

Sinek, Simon, *Start with Why?* TEDTalk Presentation (Short Version)

https://www.youtube.com/watch?v=IPYeCltXpxw

A great video that explains why some companies enjoy outrageous success and others do not. We as marketers are essentially companies ourselves (YOU, Inc.), and this is an excellent portrayal of how we should all aspire to handle our referral sources.

ABOUT THE AUTHOR

Howard J. Manns has been in leadership roles in advertising and marketing for over 30 years. In the past 12 years he has focused on healthcare marketing and operations and has served as a regional marketing director, administrator and consultant in the long-term care arena.

With the inception of Professional Healthcare Development, Howard has been able to expound his philosophy of tapping into the inner energy of leadership in all of us. He draws from his knowledge and life-experience to educate and motivate those who desire to increase their potential. Leadership is not the title you hold; it is the person you are and the way you influence people.

As a motivational speaker, Howard conducts enlightening, informational and inspirational lectures tailored to his audience. Participants have noted that his presentations are humorous, memorable and hold lasting value. They walk away with a renewed sense of enthusiasm for their careers, their relationships and their lives.

www.ingramcontent.com/pod-product-compliance
Lightning Source LLC
Chambersburg PA
CBHW050355280326
41933CB00010BA/1471

* 9 7 8 0 9 9 0 6 2 0 1 0 5 *